With love to our little angel, Zach
~ Mimi

THE WISE ANIMAL HANDBOOK

Kate B. Jerome

ARCADIA KIDS

Attempt new skills from time to time.

Just **try** to think them **through.**

And if you find you're left behind...

...then change your point of view.

Try not to **think** of just yourself.

Invent new ways to share.

Stay close to **friends** whom you can **trust.**

But
always
be
aware.

Avoid
the
tattle
in the
tale.

Insist that truth is best.

Embrace with pride the strengths you have.

Demand
to be
impressed.

Enjoy the peace that nature brings.

Ignore what's just for show.

Join forces when the road gets rough.

Admit when you don't know.

Remember
family
is the
best.

Despite the ups and downs.

Don't **hide** from things that you must **face.**

Make
joyful
laughing
sounds.

Eat **healthy** food to **grow** up **strong.**

Be **patient** with your friends.

Try not to take a stubborn stand.

Be **quick** to make amends.

Excuse
yourself
when
manners
slip.

Be helpful every day.

Keep **trying** even when it's **hard.**

But don't forget to play!

And
sing

...and **dance** each **day!**

Written by Kate B. Jerome
Design and Production: Lumina Datamatics, Inc.
Coloring Illustrations: Tom Pounders
Research: Eric Nyquist

Cover Images: See back cover

Interior Images: 002 Anetapics/Shutterstock.com; 003 George Green/Shutterstock.com; 004 Sergey Uryadnikov/Shutterstock.com; 005 Gnomeandi/Shutterstock.com; 006 Bruce MacQueen/Shutterstock.com; 007 Henk Bentlage/Shutterstock.com; 008 M.M./Shutterstock.com; 009 Mikael Damkier/Shutterstock.com; 010 Brendan van Son/Shutterstock.com; 011 Michael Pettigrew/Shutterstock.com; 012 StevenRussellSmithPhotos/Shutterstock.com; 013 Pakhnyushchy/Shutterstock.com; 014 Patjo/Shutterstock.com; 015 Quinn Martin/Shutterstock.com; 016 Lincoln Rogers/Shutterstock.com; 017 Dirk Ercken/Shutterstock.com; 018 Karel Gallas/Shutterstock.com; 019 Orangecrush/Shutterstock.com; 020 Guenter-foto/Shutterstock.com; 021 Janecat/Shutterstock.com; 022 Shironina/Shutterstock.com; 023 Annette Shaff/Shutterstock.com; 024 Vitaly Titov/Shutterstock.com; 025 Rohappy/Shutterstock.com; 026 MattiaATH/Shutterstock.com; 027 Otsphoto/Shutterstock.com; 028 FikMik/Shutterstock.com; 029 Four Oaks/Shutterstock.com; 030 Ekaterina Kolomeets/Shutterstock.com; 031 Hugh Lansdown/Shutterstock.com.

Published by Arcadia Kids, a division of Arcadia Publishing and
The History Press, Charleston, SC

For all general information contact Arcadia Publishing at:
Telephone: 843-853-2070
Email: sales@arcadiapublishing.com

For Customer Service and Orders:
Toll Free: 1-888-313-2665
Visit us on the Internet at www.arcadiapublishing.com

Library of Congress Cataloging-in-Publication data is on file with the publisher.

Printed in China

Virginia State Insect

Eastern Tiger Swallowtail

Read Together

The eastern tiger swallowtail became the state insect in 1991. It can be found fluttering across the state from April to October.

Virginia State Bird

Northern Cardinal

Read Together

The northern cardinal was named the state bird in 1950. This bird is not only popular in Virginia. Seven other states have also named it their own state bird.

Virginia State Reptile

Eastern Garter Snake

Read Together

The idea to make the eastern garter snake Virginia's state reptile came from an 11-year-old boy in Williamsburg. The garter snake is a friend to gardeners because it eats insects that are pests.

Virginia State Fish

Brook Trout

Read Together

The brook trout was named the state fish in 1993 and can be found in the cold mountain rivers and streams across the state.